Teams and Teamwork
Peter Honey

Many thanks to Martin Harrison for his work on the cartoons in this booklet.

To find out more about teams and teamwork visit our website www.peterhoney.com

Copyright © 2001 Peter Honey

All rights reserved. This booklet is the copyright of Peter Honey. It may not be reproduced, stored in a retrieval system, or transmitted in any form or by any means, electronic, mechanical, recording, or otherwise without prior permission of Peter Honey Publications Limited.

ISBN 1 902899 15 6

Published by Peter Honey Publications Limited

Peter Honey Publications Limited
Registered Office: 10 Linden Avenue Maidenhead Berks SL6 6HB Tel: 01628 633 946 Fax: 01628 633 262
Email: info@peterhoney.com Website: www.peterhoney.com
VAT No. 208 0664 80

Contents

Section 1: Introduction

    1.1 *What is a Team?*

    1.2 *Different Types of Teams*

    1.3 *Why Teamwork is Important*

    1.4 *The Vital Distinction between Task and Process*

    1.5 *How to Use this Booklet*

Section 2: Agreeing on the Characteristics of an Effective Team

    2.1 *Introduction*

    2.2 *Characteristics of Effective Team Checklist*

    2.3 *Your Characteristics of an Effective Team*

    2.4 *Comparing your Chosen Characteristics with those Most Often Selected by other Team Members*

    2.5 *Suggestions to Help You and Your Team Live up to the Characteristics*

Section 3: Assessing whether your Team is operating Chaotically, Formally or Skilfully

    3.1 *Introduction*

    3.2 *The Stages Teams Go Through*

    3.3 *Teamwork Check*

    3.4 *How to Score and Interpret your Assessment*

    3.5 *Suggestions for Action*

Section 4: Working out the Mix of Roles in your Team(s)

    4.1 *Introduction*

    4.2 *Team Roles Questionnaire*

    4.3 *Introduction to Team Roles*

    4.4 Scoring and Interpreting the Team Roles Questionnaire

    4.5 Suggestions for Action

    4.6 Using Learning Styles to Create an Effective Team

    4.7 Additional Suggestions on How to Value the Diversity of Ideas

Section 5: Helping Teams to Improve, Develop and Learn

    5.1 Introduction

    5.2 Reviewing the Team's Performance

    5.3 Conducting a Quick Review

    5.4 Conducting a Deeper Review

    5.5 Advice to Observers

Section 6: Advice on How to Produce a Personal Development Plan

    6.1 Introduction

    6.2 What exactly is a Personal Development Plan?

    6.3 Why Have a Personal Development Plan?

    6.4 How to Convert a Suggestion for Action into a Personal Development Plan

    6.5 An Example of a Personal Development Plan

    6.6 Your Personal Development Plan

Appendix   Notes on Verbal and Non-verbal Behaviour

Section 1: Introduction

1.1 What is a Team?

Teams are special. They differ from a mere group (a team is a group but a group is not a team) because the level of co-operation and coherence is on a higher plain. Teams accomplish more than just the sum of the individuals. The jargon word for this is synergy, which is the magic achieved when individuals, with different styles, skills and perspectives, work together and achieve much more collectively than they could separately.

As we shall see, synergy is rarely achieved in a spontaneous or accidental way. It requires a number of different factors to complement each other and the likelihood of this happening by chance is about as remote as winning the national lottery. The factors that need to gel are:

- the style of the leader
- the behaviour of the team members
- the team's working procedures
- the nature of the team's task
- the availability of relevant resources.

If one or more of these is out of kilter with the rest, then synergy will not be achieved.

1.2 Different Types of Teams

Teams come, just like people, in different shapes and sizes. There are big teams, small teams, temporary teams, permanent teams, real teams and virtual teams. There are multi-disciplinary teams, cross-functional teams and multi-national teams. There are teams that tackle complex projects of strategic importance with big budgets at their disposal and teams with the responsibility for running a unit or department smoothly on a day-to-day basis. There are teams that have to operate at the leading edge of innovation and creativity and teams that maintain and sustain processes that have already been developed.

Clearly different teams face different challenges but these tend to be differences of degree rather than of kind. The factors that determine the effectiveness of a team remain constant whatever the scale of the task.

1.3 Why Teamwork is Important

No organisation can function without teams. Even a sole-practitioner, with the exception of a hermit on a desert island, is dependent on a network of collaborative relationships. A small organisation might have only one team, of, say two or three people. A large organisation will have lots of overlapping teams with a single individual belonging to a number of different teams.

Just as mortar binds bricks together in a wall, teams are the mortar that holds an organisation together. The whole point of an organisation is to create value through operating collaboratively. The basic assumption is that 'two heads are better than one' and teams are the way this is translated into practice.

Teamwork has always been an important contributor to effectiveness and productivity. Recent changes in many organisations have tended to accentuate this. The whole empowerment movement, for example, together with reductions in hierarchical levels and functional barriers, rests on the assumption that teamwork, often cross-functional and multi-disciplinary, will produce the goods.

1.4 The Vital Distinction between Task and Process

Task is the word used to describe *what* a team has to do. Tasks might be to review progress, plan a piece of action, analyse a problem or to decide on the best way forward. Achieving the task is top priority.

Process, on the other hand, is the word used to describe *how* the team is tackling the task. If tasks are ends, processes are means. Process is important because it helps or hinders the achievement of the team's task.

Process might be agreeing on a common understanding of the objectives, deciding in which order to do things, allocating time slots for different activities, deciding who does what and generally organising the way the team members will work together.

These two elements, task and process, are always present. You can't have one without the other. However, they are not always given the same amount of attention. Often teams are task-mesmerised and focus on the 'what' to the detriment of the 'how'. Sometimes, when teams get bogged down in procedural wrangling, the hows take precedence over the whats and the end result is put in jeopardy.

One of the toughest challenges facing teams is to strike a healthy balance between the demands of the task and the demands of the process. In this booklet more attention will be placed on process than on task, simply because this is the element that is most often underestimated. The key to superb task performance lies in the processes. Of the five factors listed on page 1, three were about process (the style of the leader, the behaviour of the team members, the team's working procedures). Putting it another way: 60 percent of a team's success depends on sound processes and only 40 percent on having a feasible task and adequate resources.

1.5 How to Use this Booklet

This booklet is written as a resource to help you, a team member, know what to do to create a successful team. The sections that follow focus on different aspects:

Section 2:   Agreeing on the Characteristics of an Effective Team

Section 3:   Assessing whether Your Team is operating Chaotically, Formally or Skilfully

Section 4:   Working out the Mix of Roles in your Team(s)

Section 5:   Helping Teams to Improve, Develop and Learn

Section 6:   Advice on How to Produce a Personal Development Plan

Appendix: Notes on Verbal and Non-verbal Behaviour

All the materials can either be used by you as an interested individual to find out how to become a more effective participant in teams you belong to, or, better still, worked through with other team members as part of a communal team-building process.

Section 2: Agreeing on the Characteristics of an Effective Team

2.1 Introduction

Everyone has a vision of how a truly effective team would perform. The problem is that these visions tend to differ from person to person and are usually left unspoken. The more 'task mesmerised' a team, the less likely it is that time will be allocated to exploring and agreeing a shared vision. Of course, agreeing a vision does not in itself create an effective team, but it is certainly an invaluable first step. It helps enormously if people who are going to work together share some relevant values and priorities and, almost as important, understand and respect their differences.

Everyone has a vision of how a truly effective team would perform.

Starting with a blank sheet of paper is a difficult way to 'surface' different ideas on what constitutes an effective team. An easier way is to have some suggestions that you can accept reject or modify - or you can use your own ideas. That is exactly what this section provides with a checklist of potential characteristics of an effective team. You can either work through the checklist as an individual or do it as a collective exercise with your team colleagues. Either way it will help to clarify your views about the essential ingredients of successful teams. Clearly, using the checklist as the basis for striking agreements in the teams to which you belong is potentially more powerful than doing it on your own. The checklist is especially useful for newly formed teams.

If you tackle it as a team this is the recommended sequence of events:

1. Everyone does the checklist exercise individually without conferring. Allow approximately 20 minutes.

2. Everyone confers with the objective of agreeing on 12 characteristics that everyone subscribes to. Allow approximately 30-40 minutes for this (it might take longer if individuals hold strong views that don't coincide!).

3. Once the 12 characteristics have been chosen, compare your choices with those of other teams (see pages 9-11). Reconsider your chosen items only if benchmarking has raised doubts or triggered any second thoughts. Allow approximately 15 minutes for this – but longer if you revisit your earlier decisions.

4. Now comes the difficult bit. Work out what to do to ensure the team 'walks the talk' and lives up to the chosen characteristics. Some suggestions on how to go about this are given on page 12. Allow approximately 30-45 minutes for this so that you have sufficient time to produce a robust, implementable plan.

2.2 Characteristics of Effective Teams Checklist

Here are 48 statements describing different aspects of effective teamwork. They are in no order of importance. All you have to do is decide which items are, in your opinion, critically important for effective teamwork, important but not critical, and those that you consider less important. Mark the appropriate box beside each statement.

(After you have done this, you will be asked to select the most important 12 statements from those you marked as 'critical'.)

		Critical	Very important	Less important
1	There is shared understanding of the team's aims/objectives.	☐	☐	☐
2	Team members support team decisions once they have been made.	☐	☐	☐
3	The team leader ensures people do not interrupt one another.	☐	☐	☐
4	The level of mutual respect/trust is high.	☐	☐	☐
5	The team addresses disagreements and conflicts constructively.	☐	☐	☐
6	The team balances concern for processes (the 'how') with concern for the task (the 'what').	☐	☐	☐
7	Information is readily swapped/exchanged/shared between team members.	☐	☐	☐
8	The team agrees challenging objectives.	☐	☐	☐
9	The team is empowered (ie has the freedom to make and implement decisions).	☐	☐	☐
10	Team members are open and honest with each other.	☐	☐	☐
11	All the team members are active participants in the team's activities.	☐	☐	☐
12	The team is clear what is expected of it.	☐	☐	☐
13	The team's actions are consistent with its words.	☐	☐	☐
14	The team uses a systematic decision-making process.	☐	☐	☐

Not to be photocopied © *Peter Honey*

		Critical	Very important	Less important
15	The team leader facilitates, rather than directs, team discussions.	☐	☐	☐
16	The team thrives more on the differences between people than the similarities.	☐	☐	☐
17	Ideas are actively listened to and developed.	☐	☐	☐
18	The team sets high standards for itself.	☐	☐	☐
19	Different team members take the lead at different times.	☐	☐	☐
20	Team members learn from each other.	☐	☐	☐
21	The team leader keeps the discussion focused (ie relevant and to the point).	☐	☐	☐
22	The team has fun.	☐	☐	☐
23	The team comprises a diverse mixture of people eg different backgrounds, skills, points of view etc).	☐	☐	☐
24	The team has a high success rate (ie more often than not it achieves what it set out to do).	☐	☐	☐
25	Team members listen to each other.	☐	☐	☐
26	Participation levels are more or less equal (ie no one is too verbose, no one too quiet).	☐	☐	☐
27	The team weighs up the pros and cons of different courses of action before deciding the best way forward.	☐	☐	☐
28	Ideas and suggestions are actively sought from all the team members.	☐	☐	☐
29	Decisions are reached by a consensus (not by voting).	☐	☐	☐
30	The team reviews its performance/continuously improves.	☐	☐	☐
31	Each team member shares responsibility and accountability for the team's performance.	☐	☐	☐
32	The team has a leader who focuses more on the team's processes (the 'hows') than on the task (the 'what').	☐	☐	☐
33	The team creates a supportive atmosphere where team members are happy to experiment/take risks.	☐	☐	☐

Not to be photocopied © Peter Honey

		Critical	Very important	Less important
34	The team breaks down tasks into phases with an estimate of how long each will take.	☐	☐	☐
35	The team produces results within the time allocated.	☐	☐	☐
36	The team's mistakes are used as learning opportunities.	☐	☐	☐
37	The leader summarises frequently to check common understanding.	☐	☐	☐
38	The team achieves synergy (ie it produces more than the sum of the individuals).	☐	☐	☐
39	The team respects and listens to minority opinions.	☐	☐	☐
40	Team members keep their commitments to each other.	☐	☐	☐
41	Innovative suggestions are given full consideration.	☐	☐	☐
42	The team leader intervenes if the team gets side-tracked.	☐	☐	☐
43	Differences of opinion are aired and talked through to resolution.	☐	☐	☐
44	The team's successes are celebrated (and learned from).	☐	☐	☐
45	The team generates lots of creative ideas.	☐	☐	☐
46	The team members behave in co-operative ways.	☐	☐	☐
47	The team uses every opportunity to share its best practices with other teams.	☐	☐	☐
48	Team members give each other helpful feedback.	☐	☐	☐

Not to be photocopied © *Peter Honey*

2.3 Your Characteristics of an Effective Team

Now choose 12 of your 'critical' statements that, for you, capture the essence of effective teamwork.

I believe the following are essential characteristics of an effective team…

1
2
3
4
5
6
7
8
9
10
11
12

2.4 Comparing your Chosen Characteristics with Those Most Often Selected by other Team Members

The items you and your colleagues select are a matter of opinion. The important thing is to have done some hard thinking and talking about the characteristics of an effective team. This will result in a shared understanding of what the team should aspire to.

However, if you want to 'benchmark' your decisions against the selections made by other people/teams, here are the items in descending order of popularity as judged by over 150 people in over 20 different teams.

Most Popular Items

4   The level of mutual respect/trust is high.

6   The team balances concern for processes (the 'how') with concern for the task (the 'what').

8   The team agrees challenging objectives.

9   The team is empowered (ie has the freedom to make and implement decisions).

10 Team members are open and honest with each other.

11 All the team members are active participants in the team's activities.

15 The team leader facilitates, rather than directs, team discussions.

16 The team thrives more on the differences between people than the similarities.

17 Ideas are actively listened to and developed.

24 The team has a high success rate (ie more often than not it achieves what it set out to do).

30 The team reviews its performance/continuously improves.

31 Each team member shares responsibility and accountability for the team's performance.

32 The team has a leader who focuses more on the team's processes (the 'hows') than on the task (the 'what').

33 The team creates a supportive atmosphere where team members are happy to experiment/take risks.

35 The team produces results within the time allocated.

38 The team achieves synergy (ie it produces more than the sum of the individuals).

Next Most Popular Items

2   Team members support team decisions once they have been made.

7   Information is readily swapped/exchanged/shared between team members.

12 The team is clear what is expected of it.

13 The team's actions are consistent with its words.

14 The team uses a systematic decision-making process.

18 The team sets high standards for itself.

20 Team members learn from each other.

22 The team has fun.

25 Team members listen to each other.

37 The leader summarises frequently to check common understanding.

41 Innovative suggestions are given full consideration.

43 Differences of opinion are aired and talked through to resolution.

Least Popular Items

1   There is shared understanding of the team's aims/objectives.

3   The team leader ensures people do not interrupt one another.

5   The team addresses disagreements and conflicts constructively.

19 Different team members take the lead at different times.

21 The team leader keeps the discussion focused (ie relevant and to the point).

23 The team comprises a diverse mixture of people (eg different backgrounds, skills, points of view etc).

26 Participation levels are more or less equal (ie no one is too verbose, no one too quiet).

27 The team weighs up the pros and cons of different courses of action before deciding the best way forward.

28 Ideas and suggestions are actively sought from all the team members.

29 Decisions are reached by a consensus (not by voting).

34 The team breaks down tasks into phases with an estimate of how long each will take.

36 The team's mistakes are used as learning opportunities.

39 The team respects and listens to minority opinions.

40 Team members keep their commitments to each other.

42 The team leader intervenes if the team gets side-tracked.

44 The team's successes are celebrated (and learned from).

45 The team generates lots of creative ideas.

46 The team members behave in co-operative ways.

47 The team uses every opportunity to share its best practices with other teams.

48 Team members give each other helpful feedback.

2.5 Suggestions to Help You and Your Team Live Up to the Characteristics

Having spent time selecting the 12 most important characteristics, there are two major implications.

Firstly, for you personally. Working through the list of characteristics will have crystallised your thinking about effective teamwork. You now have a template against which to assess the different teams in which you participate. You could even write out your own personal list of critical characteristics ready to share with colleagues whenever you join a new team or on other occasions when airing such things could be helpful.

Secondly, when tackled as a participative exercise by a team – especially a newly formed team – discussion of the items in the list can provide a firm platform upon which to build the team's success. The very fact that these things are rarely explored makes it a novel experience for most people.

Once the 12 characteristics for effective teamwork have been selected, round off the session by taking each characteristic in turn and planning how to get it to happen. A good question to ask is 'How shall we walk the talk? What process or procedure needs to be put in place to ensure we live up to this and operate as an effective team?'

Good questions to resolve (but the relevance of these will vary depending on which characteristics have been deemed to be critical) are:

- Specifically, what do we want the person in the leadership role to do? What are his/her terms of reference?
- How shall we ensure ideas are plentiful and actively considered?
- What shall we do to kick-start co-operative behaviour?
- How shall we make learning and continuous improvement a high priority?
- What shall we do to create a supportive trustful 'culture'?
- How shall we reach collective decisions that stick?
- What shall we do to agree objectives that are challenging yet realistic?
- How shall we manage our time?
- How shall we achieve a balance between being task-focused and process-focused?
- How are we going to resolve conflicts and differences of opinion?
- What shall we do to ensure ownership of the team's work and the sharing of responsibility/ accountability?
- How shall we make it as likely as possible that working together will not only be productive, but also fulfilling and fun?

Section 3: Assessing whether your Team is operating Chaotically, Formally or Skilfully

3.1 Introduction

Teams don't just happen – they evolve. You may have heard the evolutionary process described as forming, norming, storming and performing. A more accurate description is the one we use in this section: chaotic, formal and skilful. As we shall see, it isn't necessary to have a chaotic stage at all. A team, even a new one comprised of people who haven't previously worked together, can choose to start in the formal stage and progress from there. The formal stage is the gateway to the skilful stage.

The temptation to leapfrog any formalities and go straight to the skilful stage is understandably strong. However, without the solid platform that formal ways of working establish, this tends to be illusionary. Ostensibly 'skilful' ways of working can rapidly degenerate into chaotic ways of working! Sustained skilfulness can not be achieved in one bound and can never be taken for granted.

This section contains a quick 'health check' on the way your team is performing. Once again, you can either complete the assessment yourself as a clandestine activity or you can work through it with your colleagues as a teambuilding exercise. The latter is likely to be more useful than the former because it will allow different perceptions to surface and a good dialogue to ensue. Talking through any differences, and agreeing on the best way forward, is the key to building an effective team.

Teams don't just happen - they evolve.

When using the health check as a team exercise, this is the recommended sequence of events:

1. Everyone completes and scores the 'health check' individually without conferring. Allow 5-10 minutes.

2. Everyone compares responses and has a chance to explain why they responded as they did. Encourage colleagues to give specific examples to illustrate their reasons for rating the team's performance as they have. Some specifics are helpful in sorting out any misunderstandings/differences of perception. Allow 15-20 minutes depending on how many differences have to be talked through.

3. Finally, agree what needs to be done to progress the team from chaotic to formal or from formal to skilful. Consult the ten steps (pages 21-26) to see if there are ideas you could plagiarise and/or modify. Allow 30 minutes for this (less if agreement is easily reached).

3.2 The Stages Teams Go Through

Groups become teams by progressing through a three-stage evolutionary process:

Stage 1 - The Chaotic Stage

People who are thrown together and given a task to tackle tend to underestimate the complexities of getting a team to cohere.

This is especially true if the team starts from scratch with no designated roles or previous experience of working together.

A team in the chaotic stage tries to overcome uncertainty and ambiguity by flinging itself headlong into the task in hand without giving enough, if any, attention to the process. The most noticeable characteristics of a team in the chaotic stage are as follows:

- No time given to setting clear objectives that everyone subscribes to. The team assumes that everyone knows what the objectives are.
-Ractices Inadequate time given to planning how to tackle the task.
- If a leader is appointed, no thought is given to clarifying the role and it is likely that the leader will try to impose his/her authority on a team who will not accept it.
- Ideas will be voiced but not listened to and developed. Alternatively, ideas will be rejected because the level of interruption and over speaking will be unacceptably high.

- The success of the team will be patchy. Sometimes, despite the chaos, they will get by; sometimes they will fail. Whatever the outcome, the tendency to rationalise, ie to claim they did achieve what they set out to, is high.

Stage 2 - The Formal Stage

Eventually a team will react against the chaotic stage by tightening up and becoming more formal. They are very likely to overreact, however, and introduce formal procedures that swing the pendulum too far the other way. The most noticeable characteristics of a team in the formal stage are as follows:

- There will be rigid, step-by-step procedures for agreeing objectives and plans. Typically a team might have a system of going round the table giving everyone a say. They might also instigate a system whereby the objective is written up in large letters for all to see.
- The need for strong leadership is frequently emphasised. Strong leadership in a formal team means ensuring that people stick to the procedures, don't argue, don't interrupt one another, speak 'through the chair' and so on. Strong leadership is seen as the solution to the problems of the chaotic stage. If the team fails, the leader is criticised for not being strong enough!
- Different people in the team will be given specific roles, such as time keeper or secretary, and there will be explicit rules of behaviour such as only speaking through the chair, considering one idea at a time, recapping frequently from the secretary's minutes etc.

Stage 3 - The Skilful Stage

Gradually a team outlives the formal stage and begins to 'take liberties' with its own procedures without slipping back into chaos. Sometimes a team rebels against the rigidity of the formal stage too early and might alternate between the chaotic and formal stages. Sometimes a team gets stuck in the formal stage, convinced that formality and rules are the only antidote to chaos.

The breakthrough to the skilful stage usually occurs when team members realise that some part of their formal procedures are inappropriate to the particular task in hand. They therefore cut some corners and in so doing discover that they can cope.

The most noticeable characteristics of a team in the skilful stage are as follows:

- All procedures for objective setting, planning, time keeping or whatever are agreed in the light of the task to be done and the situation. The procedures are therefore flexible rather than rigid.
- The leader is less directive and more participative.
- Group members, in whatever role, share equal responsibility for the team's success.
- The atmosphere in the team is trusting and co-operative.
- The team is more successful in achieving challenging objectives.

One of the interesting discoveries about this evolutionary process is that a team operating at a skilful stage gets there via the formal stage. Just as a caterpillar is a prerequisite to a butterfly, the formal stage seems to be a necessary developmental step to the skilful stage. The skills acquired from rigid planning are different in degree, not in kind, from the skills required for flexible planning.

So, the formal stage is an essential step in the learning process. It is the equivalent of learning to walk before you can run.

Now use the following checklist on the following page to help you assess where your team is in this evolutionary process.

3.3 Teamwork Check

Here are twelve statements about teamwork.

In the box beside each statement indicate, as honestly as you can, how rarely or often your team displays each tendency. Please use the following marking system:

| 1 Almost never/very seldom | 2 Seldom | 3 Occasionally | 4 Frequently | 5 Almost always/very frequently |

1. We tend to take our team objectives 'as read' and assume a shared understanding.

2. We don't have fixed procedures. We agree on them in the light of the task at hand.

3. We allocate specific roles to team members (eg leader, timekeeper, note taker and so on).

4. We tend to have set protocols to ensure things are orderly (eg that everyone gets opportunities to have their say, to minimise interruptions and so on).

5. The team leader is democratic and collaborative.

6. We are keen to get on with the task at hand and not spend too much time planning our approach.

7. We tend to generate lots of ideas but many get lost because we fail to listen to them and/or reject them out of hand.

8. We all feel we are 'in it together' with shared responsibility for the team's success or failure.

9. We have thorough procedures for agreeing our objectives and planning our approach to tasks.

10. The team leader tries to keep order as well as contributing to the task at hand.

11. We enjoy working together - it's fun and productive.

12. The team leader ensures that we adhere to procedures, don't argue, don't interrupt and keep to the point.

Not to be photocopied © Peter Honey

3.4 How to Score and Interpret your Assessment

Indicate in the boxes below how you rated each item on the questionnaire. When you have transferred all twelve scores to the appropriate boxes, total each of the three columns.

Item	Score		Item	Score		Item	Score
1			3			2	
6			4			5	
7			9			8	
10			12			11	
Total			Total			Total	
Chaotic stage			**Formal stage**			**Skilful stage**	

The check is designed to help you to assess whether your team operates in the chaotic, formal or skilful stage. The lowest score possible for a stage is 4 (ie you decided all four descriptions almost never/very seldom happen in your team). The highest score for a stage is 20 (ie you decided all four descriptions almost always/very frequently happen in your team).

Circle your three scores on the chart below and join them up.

	Chaotic Stage	Formal Stage	Skilful Stage	
High scores	20 19 18 17 16	20 19 18 17 16	20 19 18 17 16	
Moderate scores	15 14 13 12 11 10 9	15 14 13 12 11 10 9	15 14 13 12 11 10 9	**Midpoint**
Low scores	8 7 6 5 4	8 7 6 5 4	8 7 6 5 4	

The *highest* of the three scores gives you an indication of how you perceive the current reality of your team. If your highest score is 16 or more (ie at the 75 percent level on a scale of 4 to 20) that is a particularly strong indication of the stage you think your team is in.

The *lowest* of the three scores gives you an indication of the stage your team is least like. If your lowest score is 8 or less (ie at the 25 percent level on a scale of 4 to 20) it strongly suggests that you judge that your team does not operate in this way.

Your scores may be rather similar, say, all around the midpoint of 12, or with only small differences between them. This either indicates that you have no clear perception of the way your team operates or that your team's performance is variable - sometimes chaotic, sometimes formal, sometimes skilful. If you have an inconclusive result, get other team members to do the *Teamwork Check Questionnaire* and compare results.

3.5 Suggestions for Action

Evaluate where your team is now. If your team is predominantly:

- chaotic - you need to tighten up and move to the formal stage way of working together

- formal - you need to loosen up and move to the skilful stage of working.

- skilful - you need to conduct regular process reviews in order to guard against complacency and ensure this is maintained. The peril is that skilful groups lapse and slip back into chaos.

This rather assumes that the skilful stage is an ideal that should, in all circumstances, be striven for; but this isn't always the case. If, for example, your team:

- has ambiguous 'complex' tasks to tackle
- has little relevant expertise to draw on
- has a reasonably constant core of members
- is small (say between six and nine people)
- meets frequently (say, at least fortnightly)

then the skilful way of operating is essential.

If, however, your team:

- has specific 'routine' tasks to tackle
- has plenty of relevant expertise to draw on
- has a membership that chops and changes
- is large (say, ten or more people)
- meets infrequently (say, only monthly or less)

then a formal way of working will suffice.

In any event, the formal stage is the most vital to master, either because in itself it will provide an appropriate formula for effective teamwork, or because it is an essential stepping stone *en route* to the skilful stage. Here is a tried and tested recipe for the formal stage of operating.

Ten Steps for the Formal Stage

On the following pages are ten chronological steps with 'terms of reference' for the team leader and team members. Whenever you meet, adhere to both the structure and the roles and you will enjoy the benefits of operating as a coherent team in the formal stage. When you have accomplished this you can, if appropriate, relax formality and move on to the skilful stage.

1 Agree an Objective

Structure	Agree a specific objective (ie the desired end result) for the team meeting, eg 'By the end of this meeting we will have agreed a plan/made a decision/solved a problem.'
Team Leader's Role	Start the meeting by clarifying your understanding of the objective and checking that all team members share a common understanding.
	Modify the objective to incorporate their views.
	Ensure the agreed objective is displayed on a flipchart where it can be seen throughout the meeting.
Team Member's Role	Scrutinise the objective for the meeting to make sure
	• it pinpoints the end result for the meeting
	• it is clear and unambiguous
	• you agree with it, ie it meets your interests and expectations for the meeting.
	Ask questions of clarification and/or suggest amendments to the objective.
	When you are happy with the objective, say so.

2 Agree the Steps/Agenda for the Meeting

Structure	Clarify and agree the steps and activities (ie the agenda) to achieve the objective.
	Apportion time, in minutes, to every agenda item.
Team Leader's Role	Outline the steps necessary to achieve the objective and take the initiative in suggesting appropriate time slots for each of the remaining steps in the structure.
	If you decide to use the remaining eight steps, bear in mind that steps 3, 5, 6, 7 and 8 are likely to take longer than steps 4 and 9. Also, make sure you schedule enough time for step 10. A minimum of twenty minutes is recommended.
Team Member's Role	Carefully listen to the Team Leader's proposals on steps and timings.
	Ask questions to make sure you understand the agenda and to satisfy yourself that the timings are realistic.
	Thereafter, be time conscious and assist the Team Leader to keep to time.

3 Gather Data

Structure	Gather and share facts and opinions relevant to the objective/problem.
Team Leader's Role	Introduce this stage and make sure that key data is recorded on a flipchart.
	Encourage everyone to contribute.
	Allow questions of clarification at this stage, but prevent people prematurely coming up with ideas/suggesting solutions to the problem.
Team Member's Role	Offer whatever facts or opinions you have about the subject/problem under discussion.
	Stick to data that is relevant in the light of the objective.
	Limit yourself to questions of clarification. Do not stray into debating or suggesting solutions.

4 Check the Objective

Structure
Check that the objective for this meeting is still appropriate in the light of the data gathered in step 3.

If necessary, modify the meeting objective by making it more or less ambitious.

Team Leader's Role
Insist that the objective for this meeting is revisited to see if, now that data has been gathered, it requires any adjustment.

Remember that an objective needs to be realistic and yet challenging.

Team Member's Role
Look back at the objective and don't hesitate to suggest additions/amendments to it if the data that has been gathered changes your vision of what an appropriate objective for the meeting should be.

5 Generate Ideas

Structure
Generate ideas (ie possible courses of action).

Team Leader's Role
Introduce this stage and encourage everyone to express their ideas in an open, uninhibited way.

Get all ideas listed on flipcharts.

Avoid stating difficulties and instead encourage a positive problem-solving approach.

Team Member's Role
Offer your ideas, even half-formed ones. Insist they are written down as you intended.

Listen hard to other people's ideas and add to/develop them.

At this stage keep your doubts and reservations to yourself.

6 Develop Criteria for Evaluating Ideas

Structure	Establish criteria for judging the merits of the different ideas.
Team Leader's Role	Introduce this stage by asking for ideas on what criteria to use to evaluate the worthwhileness of the ideas generated. Don't assume that everyone is using the same criteria - surface and get agreement on them.
Team Member's Role	Offer your ideas on suitable criteria (ie practicality, feasibility, acceptability, cost-effective, high/low risk).

7 Evaluate the Ideas

Structure	Evaluate the ideas and agree the preferred option(s) to meet the objective.
Team Leader's Role	Get the team members to apply the criteria to the ideas generated in step 5. Identify the ideas worth pursuing now. Delete ideas that are not worth pursuing. Ensure each idea is categorised.
Team Member's Role	Ruthlessly apply the criteria to the ideas saying openly and honestly how you rate each idea against the criteria. Don't acquiesce. Say what you really think.

Not to be photocopied © Peter Honey

8 Agree and Conclude

Structure	Do whatever remains to be done to accomplish the objective for the team meeting, ie • agree a plan • make a decision • solve a problem.
Team Leader's Role	Introduce this stage by referring back to the objective, to establish what remains to be done. Seek proposals and suggestions from team members on how to complete the task and achieve the objective.
Team Member's Role	Check that you are clear what remains to be done in the meeting to achieve its objective. Ask questions of clarification if this isn't totally clear to you. Produce proposals and suggestions on how to incorporate the ideas into a coherent outcome (ie plan/decision/solution).

9 Plan Implementation

Structure	Produce a plan to implement the outcome agreed in step 8
Team Leader's Role	Ask the question 'What further actions need to be taken by whom and when?' Once the plan is clear summarise to check that all team members are clear on the whats, hows, whos and whens.
Team Member's Role	Join in planning how to implement the outcome of the meeting. Err on the side of volunteering to take appropriate actions. Listen to the summary of the plan and ask questions of clarification if any parts of it are not sufficiently clear.

10 Review the Team's Performance

Structure

Review:
- the achievement of the objective
- adherence to the time plan
- use of the chronological steps
- roles of the team leader and team members.

Plan what needs to be done, and how, the next time the team works together, to create the conditions for even better teamwork.

Team Leader's Role

Introduce this stage and list, on flipcharts, team members' opinions about what went well and what could have gone better.

Encourage all team members to say what they really think (if it includes criticisms of the team leader, resist the temptation to become defensive).

Insist that just *one* improvement area is selected for attention. Invite each person to choose an issue from the lists of 'went well' and 'could have gone better' that they regard as top priority for improved teamwork.

Once the issue has been selected, gather ideas on what could be done to improve performance.

Plan exactly what to try next time the team meets.

Ensure that the plan is written on a flipchart.

Team Member's Role

Speak up and give your honest assessment of how the team performed.

Make sure that what you say is recorded correctly, either as a 'went well' or as a 'could have gone better'.

If you don't agree with someone else's view, resist the temptation to argue. Just accept it as a perception that differs from yours.

Join in the selection of one improvement area.

Produce ideas on how the team could operate better in the area chosen.

Make a personal note of the improvement plan so that you can bring it with you to the next team meeting.

Section 4: Working out the Mix of Roles in your Team(s)

…and Discovering which Role(s) you are most Comfortable with

4.1 Introduction

An effective team thrives on the diversity of its members. The greater the mix of different backgrounds, disciplines, perspectives, styles and behaviours, the greater the potential for achieving synergy where the sum of the whole exceeds the sum of the parts.

Unfortunately, too many teams are constituted from a homogenous population where people are similar in experience and outlook. Working with like minds is understandably easier than struggling to get coherence from a more diverse mix, but easier doesn't necessarily mean better.

The challenge with diverse team members is to manage them in such a way that different ideas are actively considered and not dismissed out of hand. There is more advice on how to process diverse ideas later in this section.

This section contains a self-assessment questionnaire designed to help you explore the roles you use most frequently when participating in teamwork. If all the members of a team complete the questionnaire, then the collective results can throw significant light on possible imbalances in the team which, if redressed, can significantly enhance team effectiveness.

Here is a suggested sequence of events when using the roles questionnaire as a teambuilding exercise.

1. Everyone completes the questionnaire individually without conferring. Allow approximately 10-15 minutes for this.

2. Everyone reads the descriptions of the roles (see page 33) and scores and interprets their questionnaire (page 36). Allow approximately 10 minutes for this.

3. Have a discussion where the overall results are explored. It is useful to display the results on a flipchart or white board so that they can be a reference point during the discussion. Check to see whether there are any obvious trends. For example, do the results show an imbalance between the task-oriented and process-oriented roles (see page 34)? Are

there too many leaders? Are there too few thinkers? Are there too many supporters and not enough challengers, or vice versa? Allow 30 minutes for this.

4   Finally, in the light of the overall results/trends, decide what implications they have for the team's performance. You may need, for example, to consider allocating specific roles to people who aren't necessarily comfortable with them. In the short term, this could hamper the team's performance as people learn to master an unfamiliar role. From a longer-term perspective, however, 'forcing' people to adopt roles that are normally outside their comfort zone could be an admirable way to achieve a more equitable mix of the different roles (and, at the same time, a way to provide team members with developmental opportunities). Allow approximately 30 minutes to agree an overall plan.

4.2 Team Roles Questionnaire

This questionnaire will help you to discover your style when working in a team.

Simply indicate, as honestly as you can, in the box beside each statement how rarely or often you display each tendency. Please use the following 'marking' system:

| 1 | Almost never/ very seldom | 2 | Seldom | 3 | Occasionally | 4 | Frequently | 5 | Almost always/ very frequently |

1. I tend to hold strong views on most subjects.
2. I tend to ask other people for their views.
3. I tend to get my way by pressuring people.
4. I tend to get impatient with people who take too long to get to the point.
5. I can be counted on to contribute original ideas.
6. I use humour to ease tensions and maintain good relationships.
7. Once I've reached a decision, I tend to stick to it.
8. I seek common understanding prior to making decisions.
9. I have no hesitation in objecting to others' views.
10. I urge the group to stick to plans and schedules to meet deadlines.
11. I can quickly see how to improve other people's ideas.
12. I avoid getting involved in conflict.
13. I tend to have to explain things to people.
14. I tend to modify my opinion after listening to other points of view.
15. I am quite prepared to be a minority of one if I think I'm right.
16. When things aren't progressing well, I push ahead and get the job done.

Not to be photocopied © Peter Honey

| 1 | Almost never/very seldom | 2 | Seldom | 3 | Occasionally | 4 | Frequently | 5 | Almost always/very frequently |

17. ☐ I tend to put forward lots of ideas.

18. ☐ I am ready to back a suggestion if it is in the common interest.

19. ☐ I tend to talk more than I listen.

20. ☐ I tend to ask people lots of questions.

21. ☐ I am impatient with people who are slow on the uptake (I don't suffer fools gladly).

22. ☐ I don't mind being unpopular if it gets the job done.

23. ☐ I develop other people's ideas so that they are improved.

24. ☐ I tend to solicit support from other people.

25. ☐ I tend to override opposition to my views.

26. ☐ I tend to trust other people to perform well.

27. ☐ Inefficiency makes me angry.

28. ☐ I have a reputation for having a no-nonsense, 'straight to the point' style.

29. ☐ I am careful not to jump to conclusions.

30. ☐ I tend to seek approval and support from others.

31. ☐ I pay careful attention to detail and check things to correct errors.

32. ☐ I tend to aim for consensus decisions.

33. ☐ I challenge complacency whenever I come across it.

34. ☐ I tend to be forceful and dynamic.

Not to be photocopied © *Peter Honey*

| 1 | Almost never/very seldom | 2 | Seldom | 3 | Occasionally | 4 | Frequently | 5 | Almost always/very frequently |

35. ☐ I enjoy analysing situations and weighing up alternatives.

36. ☐ I am a friendly person and find it easy to establish rapport with others.

37. ☐ I put my ideas forward strongly.

38. ☐ I map out alternatives and help other people to decide on the best course of action.

39. ☐ When things are going badly I challenge the 'system' (accepted ways of doing things, rules and procedures).

40. ☐ I press for action to make sure people don't waste time or go round in circles.

41. ☐ I like to anticipate difficulties and be prepared for them.

42. ☐ I am good at noticing when someone in the group is feeling resentful or upset.

43. ☐ I provide others with as much information as I think they need.

44. ☐ I listen carefully to what others have to say.

45. ☐ I tend to hurry people along whenever I think they are dragging their feet on something.

46. ☐ When people have doubts and second thoughts I urge them to stay resolute and to press on with the task at hand.

47. ☐ I like to ponder different options before making up my mind.

48. ☐ I can work well with a very wide range of people with different styles and personalities.

49. ☐ I continually check to see that people are doing things the way I want them done.

50. ☐ I openly communicate the whys and wherefores of a situation.

Not to be photocopied © *Peter Honey*

| 1 | Almost never/ very seldom | 2 | Seldom | 3 | Occasionally | 4 | Frequently | 5 | Almost always/ very frequently |

51. ☐ I tend to point out snags, difficulties and flaws with people's ideas.

52. ☐ In discussions, I like to get straight to the point.

53. ☐ People say I'm too analytical and cautious.

54. ☐ I put effort into fostering good working relationships.

55. ☐ I tend to tell people what needs to be done.

56. ☐ When people oppose my views I tend to question them to understand why.

57. ☐ When things aren't progressing well I challenge people to be more effective.

58. ☐ People who are flippant and don't take things seriously enough irritate me.

59. ☐ I like to think things through before doing something.

60. ☐ I tend to be open about how I'm feeling.

4.3 Introduction to Team Roles

The idea that a combination of different people working together can achieve synergy is central to the concept of a team as opposed to a mere group. People, each with different views, who fail to cohere, or who simply proceed by letting the majority view prevail (as in voting), are a group (ie a collection of individuals) not a team.

Research into the differences between successful and unsuccessful teams highlights the importance of having a mix of people with different ways of behaving. It is the combination of different roles within a team that seems a crucial factor in its success. A team benefits from the differences rather than the similarities between people. Five key roles are:

Leader	Making sure that objectives are clear and that everyone is involved and committed
Challenger	Questioning ineffectiveness and taking the lead in pressing for improvements/results
Doer	Urging the team to get on with the task in hand
Thinker	Producing carefully considered ideas and weighing up and improving ideas from other people
Supporter	Easing tensions and maintaining harmonious working relationships.

Not to be photocopied © Peter Honey

A successful team blends these different roles together so that the strengths of one compensate for the weaknesses of another. This is why a mixture of different people have the potential to dovetail and become a cohesive team. It is the Leader's job to aid and abet this dovetailing process.

A team with a mixture of roles is better equipped to strike a balance between concern for task (the 'what') and concern for process (the 'how'). This is because the Leader and Supporter roles are process-oriented whereas the Challenger and Doer roles are task-oriented. The Thinker produces task and process ideas, and is therefore a mixture of both.

Each of the team roles have characteristics that in certain circumstances are likely to be strengths and in other circumstances, weaknesses. The tables that follow give four strengths and four weaknesses for each.

Directive Leader

Strengths

Decisive

Consistent

Provides clear direction

Persuasive

Weaknesses

Stubborn

Talks too much

Overrides opposition

Doesn't trust people

Collaborative Leader

Strengths

Participative

Aims for consensus

Good listener

Good questioner

Weaknesses

Can appear indecisive/'wobbly'

Too trusting

Can be too democratic

Inappropriate leadership in a crisis/under time pressures

Challenger

Strengths

Assertive

Asks probing questions

Persistent – keeps plugging away

High standards – won't tolerate anything substandard

Weaknesses

Upsets people/ruffles feathers

Pressurises people

Can appear negative

Insensitive to people's feelings

Doer

Strengths

Businesslike

Focused on results

Resolute

No-nonsense style/approach

Weaknesses

Doesn't suffer fools gladly

Nags people

Lacks sense of humour

Thick skinned

Thinker

Strengths

Idea-haver

Builds/develops other people's ideas

Analytical

Problem-solver

Weaknesses

Worrier

Analyses to a fault

Needs time to think things through

Prefers to 'play' with ideas/options rather than close down/make a decision

Supporter

Strengths

Friendly

Open re own feelings

Sensitive to people's feelings

Good at establishing rapport with a range of different people

Weaknesses

Uncomfortable with conflict

Seeks approval

Bends with the wind

Needs to be popular/liked

4.4 Scoring and Interpreting the Team Roles Questionnaire

The *Team Roles Questionnaire* is designed to establish which of the five roles you are most comfortable with. It also sub-divides the Leader role to give you an indication of whether you tend to be a directive or collaborative leader. Transfer your marks into the boxes below.

1 ☐	2 ☐	3 ☐	4 ☐	5 ☐	6 ☐
7 ☐	8 ☐	9 ☐	10 ☐	11 ☐	12 ☐
13 ☐	14 ☐	15 ☐	16 ☐	17 ☐	18 ☐
19 ☐	20 ☐	21 ☐	22 ☐	23 ☐	24 ☐
25 ☐	26 ☐	27 ☐	28 ☐	29 ☐	30 ☐
31 ☐	32 ☐	33 ☐	34 ☐	35 ☐	36 ☐
37 ☐	38 ☐	39 ☐	40 ☐	41 ☐	42 ☐
43 ☐	44 ☐	45 ☐	46 ☐	47 ☐	48 ☐
49 ☐	50 ☐	51 ☐	52 ☐	53 ☐	54 ☐
55 ☐	56 ☐	57 ☐	58 ☐	59 ☐	60 ☐
Directive Leader	**Collaborative Leader**	**Challenger**	**Doer**	**Thinker**	**Supporter**

Enter your scores into the appropriate boxes on the table below*.

	Directive Leader	Collaborative Leader	Challenger	Doer	Thinker	Supporter
Very high scores	41-50	44-50	40-50	42-50	43-50	46-50
High scores	38-40	41-43	37-39	39-41	39-42	43-45
Moderate scores	34-37	37-40	32-36	34-38	34-38	38-42
Low scores	31-33	34-36	28-31	30-33	32-33	36-37
Very low scores	0-30	0-33	0-27	0-29	0-31	0-35

*These norms are based on the scores gained by 150 team members in a mix of different organisations and sectors.

Not to be photocopied © *Peter Honey*

4.5 Suggestions for Action

There are two quite different routes open to you depending on whether you to use the questionnaire solely as a self-development tool or whether it is going to be used collectively as a team-building exercise. Let us look at each in turn.

How to Develop your Personal Team Role Repertoire

Clearly, the broader your repertoire the better equipped you are to be an effective team member, able to turn your hand to any role as circumstances dictate.

Start by focusing on a role where you scored relatively lower than the others (this may not mean your score for this role was literally 'low' because your lowest score might have fallen in the moderate band).

Now look back at the score key to see which items within that role you scored with 1 or 2. If you wish you could also include items you scored 3 'occasionally'. The idea is to pinpoint the behaviours within a role that you only do occasionally or less and, presumably, some of these (not necessarily all) you need to concentrate on doing more often in order to bring them up into your repertoire. As always, it is more feasible to be highly selective about how many behaviours to practise simultaneously and also when to take the risks involved in behaving in uncharacteristic ways. It helps to avoid confusion, and enlists support, if you let other team members know what you are up to and why.

Another interesting possibility is to get your colleagues to complete the *Team Roles Questionnaire* to get a picture of how they perceive your behaviour in the team. You could then draw comparisons between the way you assessed yourself and the way other team members see you. If there are large discrepancies then they become the subject of further exploration and clarification before you decide what aspects to focus on in your development plan.

Having located some behaviours within a role you could do more often, you now need deliberately to indulge in them. It helps if you have colleagues in your team who can be briefed to watch for the 'fledgling' behaviours and give you supportive feedback. The act of eliciting someone's aid in this way also helps to make you more purposeful and determined. It seems silly to tell someone you are going to do something and then not do it!

How to Get a Better Mix of Roles within your Team

If your team's results reveal an imbalance of roles, you will need to agree how best to allocate different roles to different team members. This may mean some people will have to curb their natural tendencies and instead focus on a different batch of behaviours. Clearly, this is easier to achieve if the person already has some leanings towards a particular role.

Use the lists that follow as short 'job descriptions' for each role, so that people are absolutely clear what is required of them. If you have an observer (see Section 5) they can be briefed to monitor people's behaviour against the appropriate job descriptions and to give feedback.

Leader Role

Leaders employ some or all of the following behaviours. They:

- bring in group members by inviting their comments and soliciting their ideas
- clarify the group's objectives
- 'grasp the nettle' by raising issues and problems that the group ought to face and tackle
- listen to group members' opinions and check that they have been understood
- summarise at frequent intervals
- steer conversations through to consensus decisions by encouraging group members to say what they really think and genuinely agree on a course of action
- 'lead from the front' by deciding what needs to be done in difficult situations, where a consensus cannot be reached or where time is tight.

Challenger Role

Challengers employ some or all of the following behaviours. They:

- tend to get their own way by pressurising people
- have no hesitation in objecting to other people's views
- are quite prepared to be a minority of one if they think they are right
- show impatience and irritation with people who are slow on the uptake (they don't suffer fools gladly)
- become exasperated with what they regard as inefficiency
- challenge complacency whenever they come across it
- challenge the 'system' (ie accepted ways of doing things, rules and procedures)
- tend to ginger people up whenever they think they are dragging their feet on something
- tend to point out the snags and difficulties with people's ideas
- step in and take a positive lead when things aren't progressing well.

Doer Role

Doers employ some or all of the following behaviours. They:

- get impatient with people who 'beat about the bush'
- urge people to stick to plans and schedules and meet deadlines
- push ahead and get the job done when things aren't progressing well
- don't mind being unpopular if it gets the job done
- have a reputation for having a no-nonsense 'call a spade a spade' style
- tend to be forceful and dynamic
- press for action to make sure people don't waste time or go round in circles
- urge people to press on with the task in hand especially when they have second thoughts
- like to get straight to the point
- get irritated with flippant people who don't take things seriously enough.

Thinker Role

Thinkers employ some or all of the following behaviours. They:

- can be counted on to contribute original ideas
- can quickly see what is wrong with unsound ideas put forward by others
- tend to put forward lots of ideas
- develop other people's ideas so that they are improved
- are careful not to jump to conclusions too quickly
- enjoy analysing situations and weighing up alternatives
- like to anticipate probable difficulties and be prepared for them
- like to ponder alternatives before making up their minds
- have a reputation for being analytical and cautious
- like to think things through before doing something.

Supporter Role

Supporters employ some or all of the following behaviours. They:

- use behaviour to ease tensions and maintain good relationships
- avoid getting involved in conflicts
- are always ready to back a good suggestion in the common interest
- tend to change their minds after listening to other people's points of view
- tend to seek approval and support from others
- are friendly and find it easy to establish good rapport with others
- are good at noticing when someone in the group is feeling aggrieved or upset
- work well with a wide range of people
- like to foster good working relationships
- tend to be open about their feelings.

4.6 Using Learning Styles to Create an Effective Team

Learning style preferences provide another useful way to examine diversity within a team. If you are interested in this avenue of exploration, the styles (Activist, Reflector, Theorist and Pragmatist) are described in the *Learning Styles Questionnaire (80-item version)* booklet.

Basically the advice is, wherever possible, to have a mix of different learning styles within a team so that the strengths of one style compensate for the weaknesses of another style. All the research confirms that teams are best equipped to perform, deliver and learn by drawing on a blend of different styles.

4.7 Additional Suggestions on How to Value the Diversity of Ideas

As we said earlier, diverse team members have the potential to produce winning teams if, and this is an important proviso, they can rise to the challenge of respecting difference. Too much sameness results too easily in 'group think' where the range of ideas is restricted and agreements are too cosy. The cut and thrust of processing many different ideas, each with their own advantages and disadvantages, provides a team with its essential raw material. It could be argued that the whole point of teamwork is to produce more ideas than one person could on their own and to process those ideas in order to get a better result than one person could hope to achieve.

There are a number of specific things you can do to ensure ideas in your team are plentiful and flourish.

1 If you are going to brainstorm ideas remember that this will suit the more robust, ebullient team members but handicap, even exclude, quieter more thoughtful members. The answer is to give advance notice of the topic so that team members who prefer to prepare can come to the brainstorm with a ready-made list of ideas to contribute. Also, build in pauses during brainstorming so that people can look back over the ideas that have been suggested and use them as the trigger for more. From a diversity point of view, it is a mistake to conduct spontaneous brainstorming sessions.

2 Make it a rule that ideas, especially those that at first sight seem to have little merit, must never be ignored or dismissed out of hand. A useful technique is to have a rule that everyone has to react to an idea by saying a couple of things they like about it before being 'allowed' to state a concern. Also, that the concern should be expressed, not as a difficulty, but as an open-minded question with the prefix 'My concern is how to….?' This invites constructive comments that might improve the idea rather than kill it off.

3   Consult team members individually before and after team meetings. People who are inclined to feel inhibited and reluctant to speak up are often more forthcoming in one-to-one discussions. Pressures to conform, acquiesce and not lose face are inevitably greater in a team meeting.

4   When triggering ideas use a whole variety of different approaches rather than sticking to one. Here are some possibilities:

- asking open-ended questions
- asking closed questions
- floating a tentative idea and inviting reactions
- getting people to play devil's advocate with a tentative idea
- getting people to develop a tentative idea
- getting people to identify the advantages and disadvantages of a number of different ideas
- soliciting ideas from one person at a time
- brainstorming
- collecting ideas in writing anonymously
- circulating a list of ideas and getting people to put them into priority order/indicate their three favourites.

5   Place great emphasis on the need to build on ideas. This can turn the most half-baked, initially unpromising, idea into something worthwhile and workable. There is more about building and its effects on page 59.

6   Finally, err on the side of thanking people for their ideas – especially if, in the event, they failed to make the grade and were not accepted. The behaviour of idea-having needs to be recognised and reinforced regardless of the eventual outcome. This will ensure a steady flow of ideas, without which a team's potency would be seriously reduced.

Section 5: Helping Teams to Improve, Develop and Learn

5.1 Introduction

Teams often need help if continuous improvement/development is to be sustained. The help can either come from within by, for example, rotating the role of observer, or from outside by inviting someone from another team or a trainer/developer to act as observer/coach. Having a dispassionate observer may seem like a luxury – but the payoff can be enormous. Seeing the wood for the trees is far from easy when you are a full-time participant in a team's activities.

This section makes suggestions about how to structure reviews of the team's performance and gives specific advice to observers.

5.2 Reviewing the Team's Performance

Regular and frequent reviews of a team's performance are the key to continuous improvement and learning. Without thorough reviews of task achievement (the 'whats') and the processes (the 'hows') potentially valuable ideas and insights become trapped inside individuals with no opportunity to make them available to the team. It is extraordinary how often people express dissatisfaction with a team's progress in private, behind the team's back. All that is needed is a little space, time and encouragement for different views about the team's performance to be collectively aired and shared.

5.3 Conducting a Quick Review

The most straightforward (but still worthwhile) way to structure a review is as follows:

- Get someone other than the person who has chaired/led the team to facilitate the review. The team leader or champion has often been so busy during the team meeting that it is difficult for them to be sufficiently dispassionate during the review.

- Create two columns on a flipchart or whiteboard headed up:

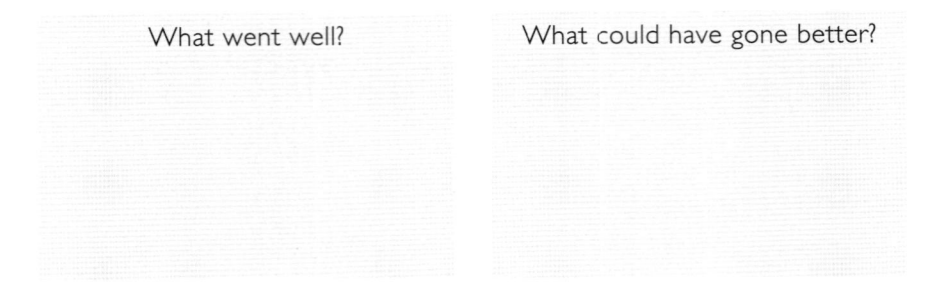

What went well?	What could have gone better?

- List all the views with minimal editing/précising.

- Say "In the light of these lists, if we could improve just *one* aspect of the team's performance, what would it be?" Collect up ideas on priority areas for improvement.

- Focus on one aspect and ask for suggestions on what could be done better, or differently, to improve the team's performance.

- Agree an improvement plan that includes what, why, how, who and when.

- Circulate an email or memo with a reminder of the improvement plan to all team members.

A basic review of this kind should take no more than 20 minutes from start to finish.

5.4 Conducting a Deeper Review

A deeper review requires more time, say, 45-60 minutes and, vitally, feedback from an observer. Anyone can become the team's designated observer. One option is to rotate the observing role so that different team members do it at different team meetings. Another option is to invite a colleague from a different team to act as observer or, even, to use an outside consultant/developer.

Whoever undertakes the role, an insider or an outsider, it must be understood that their brief is to focus on process issues, not task issues. In other words, the observer concentrates on how the team conducts itself - the aspect which is likely to receive insufficient attention as the participants engage with the task. The more challenging the task, the more likely it is to dominate and upset the task-process balance.

Once it is clear that the observer's role is to concentrate on process, the next issue, given that there are a number of different aspects to process, is what process? In order to be helpful, the process needs to match the 'maturity' of the team.

Teams tend to develop awareness of process issues in a hierarchy. Awareness of fundamental structural issues comes first followed closely by role and behavioural awareness and finally by emotional awareness, rather like building a pyramid in layers from the base up.

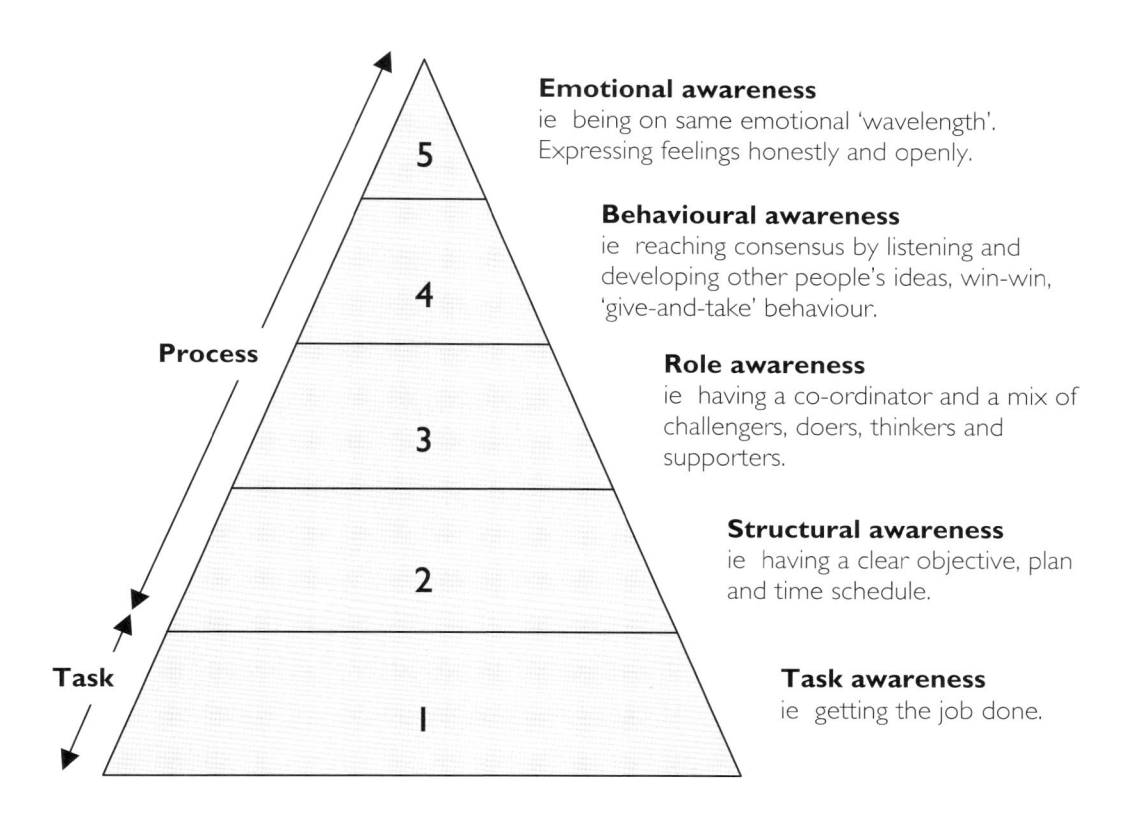

Figure 1

5 — Emotional awareness
ie being on same emotional 'wavelength'. Expressing feelings honestly and openly.

4 — Behavioural awareness
ie reaching consensus by listening and developing other people's ideas, win-win, 'give-and-take' behaviour.

3 — Role awareness
ie having a co-ordinator and a mix of challengers, doers, thinkers and supporters.

2 — Structural awareness
ie having a clear objective, plan and time schedule.

1 — Task awareness
ie getting the job done.

(Process / Task axis)

Some teams never become aware of all these process levels. They may not progress beyond a mixture of structure and roles. Other teams become more mature by developing an awareness at all levels and having the capacity to focus on a wide range of process issues depending on fluctuating needs and circumstances.

Not to be photocopied © Peter Honey

So, feedback from the observer needs to be geared to the maturity of the team. Basically a low maturity team benefits from intervention and direction and a high maturity team needs non-directive facilitation. This is a continuum with many shades of grey in between the two extremes.

Figure 2

High Maturity Team

Skilful Stage — Non-directive Feedback

8. Ask the team for ideas on what they want you to observe and feedback. You are a resource to the team seeking to understand how best you can help them.

7. Observe without intervention and give non-directive feedback by asking questions and helping the team to review their own performance.

↑

Formal Stage

6. Observe **behavioural issues** without intervention. Ask the team for their ideas on what went well/could have gone better, and then link your feedback to their perceptions.

5. Observe **role issues** without intervention. Ask the team for their ideas on what went well/could have gone better, and then link your feedback to their perceptions.

4. Observe **structural issues** without intervention. Ask the team for their ideas on what went well/could have gone better, and then link your feedback to their perceptions.

↑

Chaotic Stage — Directive Feedback

3. Observe and intervene with **process** points (coaching) and give directive feedback (guidance).

2. Observe and intervene with **task** points (coaching) and give directive feedback (guidance).

1. Tell the team what to do and how to do it. (Directive Leader)

Low Maturity Team

5.5 Advice to Observers

Observing, done properly, is a full time job with three phases. Firstly, there is the business of being a diligent observer and collecting data on the team's performance. Secondly, the data needs to be interpreted and prioritised. Thirdly, the team needs to be provided with feedback in such a way that they are helped to agree how to improve their performance. These are three distinct phases that are best kept separate. If, for example, you observe and interpret simultaneously there is a real risk of jumping to conclusions which 'contaminate' subsequent observations. Similarly, if you interpret 'on the hoof' whilst giving feedback, there is a danger that the interpretations will be superficial and suffer from inadequate reflection.

Here are some basic hints to help you with these three phases.

Phase 1 - Observing

1   Sit away from the team where you can see and hear adequately. A corner is ideal.

2   Explain your role (if this hasn't already been done) so that the team understands why you are observing, making copious notes, not saying anything etc. Do everything you can to allay suspicions and seem friendly and helpful.

3   Draw yourself a name chart.

4   Choose an approach appropriate to the maturity of the team (see Figure 2 on Page 46).

5   Decide how to make your notes, whether to use a clean sheet and let process themes emerge or whether to use a category system focused on some specific process issues. If you use a clean sheet, it is best to adopt a three column format:

Time/Name	Observation	Interpretation
Note the time occasionally and name of speaker	Use this column to record verbatim what is said (process contributions only) and for other notes on what happens.	Use this column to flag themes, categorise happenings, and note links between things.

6   Err on the side of gathering too much detail – but stick to process, don't make notes on task except where it is useful to establish a 'context' for your process observations.

7   Unless you have negotiated intervention rights, only intervene if:

  -   it is a process point you want to catch

- you have a process suggestion that you are convinced will help the team make significantly better progress than they would without it

- you can do it quickly

- you are sure no one in the team is about to make the same point.

Phase 2 - Interpreting

1. If you have to give feedback straight away, start to identify themes in the last 10 minutes or so of the team's session. Continue to keep half an ear and eye on process.

2. Use different colours or symbols to flag observations that are linked.

3. Be selective and decide on just one or two process issues to concentrate on in your feedback. The temptation to swamp the team with too much data is considerable – especially since you have been busy making all those wonderful notes!

4. When selecting your themes remember the hierarchy of awareness chart. As a general rule deal with structural issues in the first feedback session and subsequently move on to role and behavioural issues.

5. Identify specific evidence to illustrate and substantiate your chosen process issues. If you are short of time, scan your notes from back to front and this will render evidence that happened a short time ago. This is more likely to strike a chord with the team than citing something that happened much earlier.

6. In addition to your selected issues and evidence, give thought to what constructive suggestions you are going to offer to the team.

Phase 3 - Giving Feedback

1. Move over to join the team at their table. A small point but it signals the difference between observing and feeding back.

2. Agree an agenda for the feedback session. A well-tested one is as follows:

    2.1 Invite the team to compile (on flips) two lists:

    - what went well?
    - what could have gone better?

    2.2 Give your feedback to the team adding any extra points to the two lists.

2.3 Invite the team to question you about any matters arising from your feedback.

2.4 Encourage the team to select from the lists one or two issues to focus upon.

2.5 In the light of the suggested issues, gather suggestions for action.

2.6 Plan actions so that everyone involved is clear what they have to do.

3 Stick to the approach you have chosen as appropriate to the maturity of the team.

4 Try to link your feedback to the team's own observations on what went well, what could have gone better. It is better to endorse and expand what they themselves think than to launch into something quite different.

5 Discipline yourself to stick to your chosen theme or themes and resist the considerable temptation to swamp the team with data.

6 Avoid sweeping generalisations and absolute judgements and don't say anything you can't substantiate with evidence.

7 Always make some specific suggestions on what the team could do to improve. If the team did well say so and why (evidence), but always have something to suggest to help them become even better.

8 Never finish a feedback session without the group's agreement to a specific action plan.

9 Be helpful throughout the feedback session. Don't attack or daunt.

The temptation to swamp the team with too much data is considerable

Section 6: Advice on How to Produce a Personal Development Plan

6.1 Introduction

The trouble with suggestions for action, such as the ones made in this booklet, is that they are often left as suggestions and don't get translated into action. This doesn't necessarily mean that the suggestions themselves are at fault. Inevitably, suggestions are generic and can only provide you with the germ of an idea, which has to be converted into something doable in your specific circumstances. The best way to bridge the gap between a suggestion and implementation is to produce a personal development plan. The plan is the equivalent of a secure stepping stone in a stream between two banks.

Specificity is the major difference between a suggestion for action and a plan. A suggestion is relatively vague and a plan is specific. The more you dot the i's and cross the t's, the more likely you are to have a plan that can be implemented.

6.2 What exactly *is* a Personal Development Plan?

Let's take the three words one at a time.

Personal means it is yours, tailor-made to your needs and circumstances. You own the plan.

Development describes the intention. The whole idea is to develop:

- your knowledge base (what you know)
- and/or your skills/competencies/techniques (what you can do)
- and/or your attitudes/values (what you believe)
- and/or your emotions (what you feel)
- and/or your physical strength/stamina

Development is all about getting better at one or more of these. 'Getting better' is a relative term because, of course, however good you are at something, there is always room for improvement. The accent is therefore on *continuous* development. The best way to do this is to take charge of your own development. This is called self-development.

Plan means that you know exactly what you need to do, why, how and when. The more specific the plan the more likely you are to implement it. This is in contrast to an intention which, however laudable, is vague and less likely to be implemented – either at all or successfully.

6.3 Why Have a Personal Development Plan?

Producing a Personal Development Plan has a number of benefits:

- Your plan is the best way to maximise the probability that you will do something (the 'stepping stone' effect).

- Your plan forces you to prioritise and be specific about what you are going to do by when.

- Your plan makes you visualise success and work out how to assess your achievement.

- Your plans, once implemented, scream out to be reviewed and this crystallises your learning and leads you on to fresh plans and continuous development.

6.4 How to Convert a Suggestion for Action into a Personal Development Plan

Here is step-by-step advice on precisely what to do, followed by an example of a Personal Development Plan and a blank plan for you to complete.

1. Select a suggestion for action from a previous section of this booklet that appeals to you and write it down in the 'What I am going to do' box. It is best to use your own wording rather than merely copying the suggestions word for word.

2. Now think about why you want to do this – your purpose. It could be as simple as 'To improve my performance' or 'To see how it works out in practice' or 'To experiment with something I haven't tried before'. Note your purpose in the 'Why I am going to do this' box.

3. This is the step that requires the most detail so a bigger space has been provided. Describe, as precisely as possible, how you are going to do whatever you have noted in the first box. Err on the side of including too much detail because it is the 'hows' that put the heart into your plan.

4. All respectable plans are time-bound rather than being open-ended. Work out realistically when you are going to implement your plan and note this in the 'When I am going to do this' box.

5. Finally, commit yourself to a review date and an indication of how you will assess/measure your success. Put this in the final box.

6.5 An Example of a Personal Development Plan

What I am going to do

Volunteer to act as the team's challenger.

Why I am going to do this

I have two reasons:

1. *I tend to be too compliant in team meetings and need to sharpen up my challenging skills.*
2. *Our team has too many supporters and not enough challengers. I want to see whether more challenging helps or hinders the team's performance.*

How I am going to do this

At the start of the next team meeting I will immediately volunteer myself for the challenger role and will give my reasons for doing so.

I will then participate by watching out for three different sorts of openings for challenges:

1. *Whenever someone appears to be complacent or self-satisfied.*
2. *Whenever the team slips into a routine procedure/way of working that hasn't been questioned for some time.*
3. *Whenever anyone comes up with an idea that seems to be going through 'on the nod' without sufficient scrutiny.*

I will flag up each of my challenges by saying 'I want to challenge that by asking…?'

When I am going to do this

At the next team meeting on [date]

When I will review the results/how I will know I was successful

I will have been successful if I have produced at least six challenges during the meeting and if at least half of them caused a worthwhile rethink and/or resulted in an improved idea. I will review this at the end of the meeting by asking my colleagues for feedback on how efficiently I carried out the challenger role.

6.6 Your Personal Development Plan

Date Plan Made __ /__ /__

What I am going to do

Why I am going to do this

How I am going to do this

When I am going to do this

When I will review the results/how I will know I was successful

For more detailed advice on producing Personal Development Plans, with space for up to ten plans and reviews, we recommend our booklet *Personal Development Plans*, please contact us on 01628 633 946 for more details.

Not to be photocopied

© Peter Honey

Appendix: Notes on Verbal and Non-verbal Behaviour

i Introduction

It is impossible for a team to function without numerous interactions between the team members. These may be face-to-face, on the telephone or they may be indirect through, for example, emails and other modes of communication. Whatever the means, the common currency is behaviour. What team members say to each other, and *how* they say it, markedly affects how the team 'ticks'. Behaviour is often dismissed as style rather than substance, but what an effective team needs is both. Behaviour without substance is a mere façade which is soon seen through. Substance without style usually results in needless resistance and alienation.

This section, therefore, focuses on behaviour as a vital ingredient in all teamwork and gives specific advice on which behaviours are likely to stand you and your colleagues in best stead.

ii Why Behaviour?

You have probably been told to 'behave yourself' and 'be on your best behaviour' hundreds of times if not recently, then certainly when you were a child. This tends to give behaviour moralistic undertones as to whether it is good or bad, right or wrong, acceptable or unacceptable.

Here, however, the word behaviour is being used in its 'pure' sense to refer to any overt, or obvious, action. Overt actions are plain to see and include everything we say to people, as well as non-verbal movements such as facial expressions, gestures with hands and arms, and 'body language' in general. Behaviour is smiling, frowning, shaking someone's hand, giving someone 'two fingers', looking at someone when he or she is talking, doodling, agreeing, disagreeing, shouting, whispering, praising, criticising – everything. Literally all you do and anyone else does is behaviour.

The main point to grasp is that behaviour is always directly observable, unlike many accompanying underlying factors, such as motives, attitudes, beliefs and emotional feelings, which are all covert and never directly observable.

Behaviour, therefore, is rather like the tip of an iceberg.

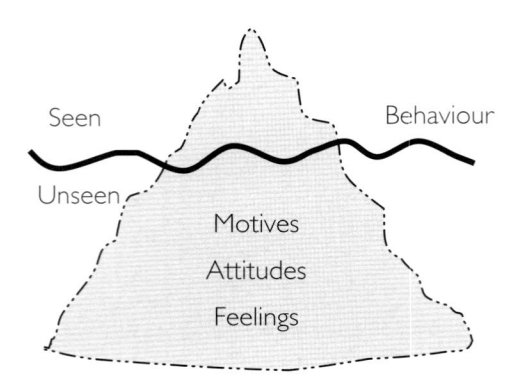

```
       Seen         Behaviour
       ~~~~~~~~~~~~~~~~~~~~~~
       Unseen
              Motives
              Attitudes
              Feelings
```

The way you behave is important because:

- The conclusions you reach about other people (ie whether you like or dislike them, trust or distrust them) are based solely on the way you see them behave (ie their actions both spoken and unspoken).
- The conclusions other people reach about you are based on the only part of you they have ready access to – your behaviour.
- In person-to-person relationships nothing is more important than behaviour. Judgements *have* to be based on it.
- Since your behaviour is so evident in a person-to-person encounter it influences (shapes) the other person's behaviour and vice versa. You can modify other people's behaviour and attitudes only through your own.

Your behaviour is, therefore, a tool that you can use to help or hinder your dealings with other people. An implication in all this is that you can change your behaviour and, via that, other people's. Since you have learned to behave the way you do now through an *ad hoc* process of learning from experience, there is no reason why you shouldn't unlearn and relearn.

When it comes to developing your own behavioural skills the following is good advice:

- put your behaviour first and your underlying attitudes and feelings second, ie smile in order to feel happy rather than smiling when you feel happy.
- set yourself specific behaviour targets and plan to expand your repertoire of behaviours.
- force yourself to behave appropriately until you have acquired the behaviour in question and no longer need consciously to force it.

iii Categories of Behaviour

People often express unease with labelling or pigeonholing human behaviour. There is, however, no alternative. The only way to make sense of behaviour is to break it down into some specifics. Every science adopts a category system and the behavioural sciences are no exception.

The advantage of using categories is that otherwise vague, global notions of behavioural differences between people can be pinpointed more precisely. This clarity helps both when observing other people's behaviour (we are less likely to succumb to the perils of jumping to a conclusion) and when planning how best to behave ourselves.

Behaviour, in common with everything else, is capable of description at different levels. There are personality-level descriptions such as extrovert and introvert. There are style-level descriptions such as autocrat and democrat and, as we saw in Section 4, there are role-level descriptions such as leader, doer, thinker, supporter.

Behaviour-level descriptions complement all these by breaking them down into smaller units (in rather the same way that Eskimos have over 50 categories to distinguish between different types of snow). Thus an autocratic style, on closer analysis, breaks down into a number of behaviours, including:

- telling rather than asking
- proposing, instructing, commanding
- interrupting, cutting people off
- disagreeing.

A democratic style, on the other hand, breaks down into some of the following behaviours:

- asking rather than telling
- suggesting
- listening, summarising back
- agreeing and checking that others agree.

iv Verbal Behaviour

Verbal behaviour covers everything you say to people either face-to-face as in a team meeting or on the telephone. This clearly covers such a vast range of possibilities that it is best to break verbal behaviour down into a number of categories and concentrate on some specifics. For convenience, verbal behaviour can be broken down into nine categories as follows:

Seeking ideas	Asking other people for their ideas.
Proposing	Putting forward ideas (possible courses of action) as statements.
Suggesting	Putting forward ideas as questions (ie 'How about doing so and so…').
Building	Developing someone else's idea.
Disagreeing	Explicitly disagreeing with something someone else has said.
Supporting	Agreeing with something someone else has said.
Difficulty stating	Pointing out the snags or difficulties with something someone else has said.
Seeking clarification/ information	Asking other people for further clarification or information.
Clarifying/explaining/ informing	Giving information, opinions and explanations.

There is nothing sacrosanct about any of these categories. They can be expanded or reduced depending on purpose and context. Behaviour categories are invaluable when it comes to planning appropriate behaviour.

Obviously what you say to another person and the way you say it will have an effect on what he or she says back as a response. The 'chemistry' of different verbal behaviours in interaction with one another has been carefully investigated; here are some of the findings, together with their implications for you.

Seeking ideas ➞ Proposing 60%   Suggesting 19%

Seeking ideas is a powerful behaviour. Nine times out of ten it is successful in provoking some ideas from the other person. It is a helpful behaviour to use whenever you need to pick someone else's brains.

Proposing → Difficulty stating 39%   Supporting 25%   Seeking clarification/information 16%

Unfortunately, proposing ideas provokes difficulties or objections more often than it wins support. If you want to 'flush out' people's reservations, then proposing is a good behaviour to use. If, on the other hand, you want to make it more likely that there will be agreement to your idea, then the next behaviour is a safer bet.

Suggesting → Supporting 42%   Difficulty stating 18%   Seeking clarification/information 17%   Building 11%

Suggesting ideas is a more effective way of gaining agreement than proposing ideas. There are, of course, no guarantees that it will succeed, because your idea may be such a rotten one that, even though it is suggested, it runs into difficulties. The actual statistics reveal that four times out of ten a suggestion is followed by an agreement, and that isn't a bad hit rate.

Building → Seeking clarification/information 17%   Supporting 32%   Building 15%   Difficulty stating 11%

Building on someone else's idea is a powerful way to get their wholehearted support. Despite this, building is a fairly rare behaviour. It seems that people find it easier to find fault with ideas than to build them up into something better. This is a good example of having a choice. People who think about their behaviour are more likely to try building than people who are in the habit of immediately criticising ideas. The fact that seeking clarification is so prevalent reminds us what a potentially confusing behaviour building can be. The lesson is to 'flag' building so that people are in no doubt, because then supporting and more building will be the most likely reactions.

Disagreeing → Clarifying/explaining/informing 42%   Disagreeing 31%   Seeking clarification/information 10%

Disagreeing on seven out of ten occasions triggers a defensive reaction or even further disagreements. It is interesting how often people get locked into a disagreeing 'spiral', where one disagreement breeds another which, in turn, breeds another and so on. Disagreeing is very much a last resort. It is best to try some of the more constructive points first.

Supporting → Clarifying/explaining/informing 33%   Proposing 29%   Suggesting 21%

Agreeing with something that someone else has said is a powerful way to encourage them to go on and say more. Eight times out of ten this will be the effect. Agreeing is, therefore, a useful behaviour if you want to gain more information from the other person. It isn't an appropriate behaviour if you want them to shut up.

Difficulty stating → Clarifying/explaining/informing 18%   Proposing 17%   Disagreeing 15%   Seeking clarification/information 12%   Seeking ideas 11%   Suggesting 10%

Pointing out difficulties is a very common behaviour but is one of the riskier ones, because research shows that it is far from certain how people will take it. Marginally, the most likely reaction is to offer some clarification or explanation. However, people often take umbrage and start disagreeing or, if you persist with difficulties, may give up and go and find someone more positive to talk to. You should watch carefully to see whether pointing out difficulties is hindering or helping the proceedings.

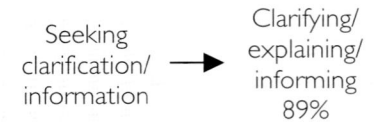

Seeking clarification/information → Clarifying/explaining/informing 89%

No surprises here. If you ask for clarification then nine times out of ten you will get it. Seeking clarification is a frequent behaviour that exerts a powerful influence over the behaviour of the other person. It is a very useful behaviour when trying to get to the bottom of things and when you need to tease information out of the other person.

| Clarifying/ explaining/ informing | Clarifying/ explaining/ informing 42% | Seeking clarification 31% | Difficulty stating 15% | Supporting 10% |

Informing is the behaviour that happens more often than any other in conversation between people. This isn't surprising, of course, because the overall purpose of talking with someone is to impart information of some kind. The most interesting aspect is how information breeds informing, which breeds informing and so on, in what can be a time-consuming loop. Sometimes this is appropriate and necessary. At other times the loop amounts to going round in circles and getting nowhere fast.

The reason why people often prolong the informing loop is because it is a relatively 'safe' way to pass the time. When you offer a piece of information, you don't commit yourself in quite the same way as when you propose or suggest an idea.

The lesson from all this? Simply that the behaviours you use have known shaping effects on the behaviours you get back from other people. The data underline the fact that you are more likely to succeed with people if you think about your behaviour and select and use behaviours that help rather than hinder progress towards your objective. This process is enhanced still further if you adopt visual behaviours that reinforce the things you are saying. It is the combination of verbal and visual that has the desired effect.

v Non-verbal Behaviour

Non-verbal or visual behaviour also has a category system, which covers a wide range of different aspects including:

- facial expressions
- eyes
- hand movements
- leg movements
- body posture
- spatial distance and orientation

In addition, there are some fringe areas such as clothes, physique and general appearance.

There is overwhelming evidence from many research studies to show that visual behaviours play a larger part in communications between people than is usually supposed.

It seems that, without necessarily being able to describe how they do it, people make judgements and form impressions based on the visual behaviours they see other people using. Perhaps the most dramatic example of this is when people meet for the first time. Within seconds, visual behaviours are sending signals that create a favourable or an unfavourable impression. Initial judgements are formed about whether the other person is friendly or unfriendly, confident or timid, trustworthy or untrustworthy, nice or nasty. Sometimes these first impressions are so strong that they stubbornly linger and defy revision, even when different signals are being transmitted by subsequent visual behaviours.

Clearly the great advantage of thinking about your visual as well as your verbal behaviour is that you can choose visual behaviours that help rather than hinder progress towards your objective. You may be in the habit of using some visual behaviours that run the risk of giving the other person a poor impression of you. The secret of success is to concentrate on some simple combinations. If you do just one thing in isolation it will probably not have the desired effect, because people gain an overall impression from a combination of:

- your facial expression and head movements
- gestures with your hands and arms
- the rest of your body, including your legs.

All three aspects need to be practised so that they all come together to give the right impression.

...people make judgements and form impressions based on the visual behaviours they see other people using.

Here are some combinations of visual behaviours. Practise doing fewer of the ones on the left and more of the ones on the right.

	People will tend to see you as **defensive** if you:	You will appear **friendly** and **co-operative** if you:
Face and head	Don't look at the other person. Avoid eye contact or immediately look away when it happens.	Look at the other person's face. Smile. Nod your head as the other person is talking.
Hands and arms	Clench your hands. Cross your arms. Constantly rub an eye, nose or ear.	Have open hands. Have uncrossed arms. Put your hands to your face occasionally.
Body	Cross your legs. Lean away from the other person. Swivel your feet towards the door.	Have uncrossed legs. Lean forward slightly. Move close to the other person.

	People will tend to see you as **anxious** if you:	You will appear **confident** if you:
Face and head	Blink your eyes frequently. Lick your lips. Keep clearing your throat.	Don't blink your eyes. Look into the other person's eyes. Thrust your chin forward.
Hands and arms	Open and close your hands frequently. Put your hand over your mouth while speaking. Tug at an ear.	Keep hands away from your face. 'Steeple' your fingertips together. Have hands together behind you (if you're standing) in an 'at ease' position.
Body	Fidget in your chair. Jig your feet up and down.	Stay still, no sudden movements, no wriggling. Lean back, if seated, with legs out in front of you. Keep straight, if standing.

Not to be photocopied © Peter Honey

	People will tend to see you as **overbearing** and **aggressive** if you:	You will appear **thoughtful** if you:
Face and head	Stare at the other person. Have a wry 'I've heard it all before' type of smile. Raise your eyebrows in amazement or disbelief. Look over the top of your glasses.	When listening, look at the other person for about three-quarters of the time. Tilt your head to one side slightly.
Hands and arms	Point your finger at the other person. Thump your fist on the table. Rub the back of your neck.	Slowly stroke your chin or the bridge of your nose. If you wear glasses, take them off and put an ear frame in your mouth.
Body	Stand while the other person remains seated. Stride around. Lean right back, if seated, with both hands behind your head and legs splayed out in front of you.	Lean forward to speak. Lean back to listen. Keep your legs still (no jiggling).

Non-verbal behaviours should accompany and reinforce what you are saying – your verbal behaviour. It is the combination of verbal and non-verbal that is likely to have the desired effect. Appropriate behaviours are the life-blood of an effective team. Without them teamwork would be non-existent.

January
Januar Janvier Enero

6	7	8	9	10	11	12
Monday *Montag Lundi Lunes*	**Tuesday** *Dienstag Mardi Martes*	**Wednesday** ☾ *Mittwoch Mercredi Miércoles*	**Thursday** *Donnerstag Jeudi Jueves*	**Friday** *Freitag Vendredi Viernes*	**Saturday** *Samstag Samedi Sábado*	**Sunday** *Sonntag Dimanche Domingo*

Atagoshita and Yabu Lane, 12–1857

Week 2

December / January
Dezember Décembre Diciembre / Januar Janvier Enero

30	31	1	2	3	4	5
Monday Montag Lundi Lunes	**Tuesday** Dienstag Mardi Martes	**Wednesday** ● Mittwoch Mercredi Miércoles	**Thursday** Donnerstag Jeudi Jueves	**Friday** Freitag Vendredi Viernes	**Saturday** Samstag Samedi Sábado	**Sunday** Sonntag Dimanche Domingo

Fukagawa Susaki and Jūmantsubo, 5–1857

Week 1